Biogr

James Egan was born in in Portarlington, Co. Laois in most of his life. In 2008, Ja studied in Oxford. James married his wife in 2012 and currently lives in Havant in Hampshire. James was a volunteer for the Halow charity for disabled young people in Guildford. James had his first book, 365 Ways to Stop Sabotaging Your Life published in 2014.

Books by James Egan

Fiction
Fairytale (A children's play)
Inherit the Earth

Non-fiction
500 Facts About Superheroes
100 Classic Stories That Aren't True
Words That Need to Exist in English
The Pocketbook of Phobias
365 Ways to Stop Sabotaging Your Life
500 Things People Believe That Aren't True
1000 Things People Believe That Aren't True
1000 Amazing Quotes
1000 Inspiring Quotes
1000 Quotes from Actors

1000 Historical Quotes

by

James Egan

Copyright 2015 © James Egan

All rights reserved. No part of this book may be reproduced, stored, or transmitted by any means - whether auditory, graphic, mechanical, or electronic - without write permission of both publisher and author, except in the case of brief excerpts used in critical articles and reviews. Unauthorised reproduction of any part of this work is illegal and reviews. Unauthorised reproduction of any part of this work is illegal and is punishable by law.

ISBN: 978-1-326-39405-9

Because of the dynamic nature of the Internet, any web addresses or links contain in this book may have changed since publication and may no longer be valid. The views expressed in this work are solely those of the author and do not necessarily reflect the views of the publisher, and the publisher herby disclaims any responsibility for them.

Any people depicted in stock imagery provided by Thinkstock are models, and such images are being used for illustrative purposes only.
Certain stock imagery © Thinkstock.

Lulu Publishing Services rev. date: 17/08/2015

For Neville

1 Abraham Lincoln — p10
2 Aesop — p12
3 Albert Einstein — p14
4 Aldous Huxley — p16
5 Aristotle — p18
6 Arthur Conan Doyle — p20
7 Arthur Miller — p22
8 Benjamin Franklin — p24
9 Bruce Lee — p26
10 Buddha — p28
11 Byron — p30
12 Carl Jung — p32
13 Carl Sagan — p34
14 Chankaya — p36
15 Charles Bronte — p38
16 Charles Darwin — p40
17 Charles Dickens — p42
18 Charlie Chaplin — p44
19 Confucius — p46
20 C.S. Lewis — p48
21 Dalai Lama — p50
22 Edgar Allen Poe — p52
23 Eleanor Roosevelt — p54
24 Emily Dickinson — p56
25 Ernest Hemingway — p57
26 Euripides — p59
27 Francis Bacon — p61
28 Franz Kafka — p63
29 Friedrich Nietzsche — p65
30 F. Scott Fitzgerald — p67
31 Fyodor Dostoevsky — p69
32 Galileo Galilei — p71
33 George Bernard Shaw — p73
34 George Orwell — p75
35 George Santayana — p77
36 George Washington — p79
37 Henry Ford — p81
38 Henry Ibsen — p83
39 H. G. Wells — p85
40 Hippocrates — p86
41 Homer — p88
42 Honor de Balzac — p90

43 Isaac Asimov	p92
44 Isaac Newton	p94
45 James Joyce	p96
46 Jane Austen	p98
47 Jesus Christ	p100
48 John F. Kennedy	p102
49 John Lennon	p104
50 John Milton	p106
51 John Steinbeck	p108
52 Jonathan Swift	p110
53 Joseph Campbell	p112
54 Joseph Conrad	p114
55 Jules Verne	p116
56 Julius Caesar	p118
57 Leo Tolstoy	p120
58 Lewis Carroll	p122
59 Ludwig von Beethoven	p124
60 Mahatma Gandhi	p126
61 Marcus Aurelius	p128
62 Mark Twain	p130
63 Martin Luther King	p132
64 Maya Angelou	p134
65 Michio Kaku	p136
66 Moliere	p138
67 Muhammad Ali	p140
68 Napoleon Bonaparte	p142
69 Neil deGrasse Tyson	p144
70 Oscar Wilde	p146
71 Ovid	p148
72 Plato	p149
73 Plautus	p151
74 Pliny the Elder	p153
75 Ralph Waldo Emerson	p155
76 Rene Descartes	p157
77 Richard Dawkins	p159
78 Robert Lewis Stevenson	p161
79 Salvador Dali	p162
80 Samuel Beckett	p164
81 Sigmund Freud	p166
82 Socrates	p168
83 Sophocles	p170
84 Stephen Fry	p172

85 Stephen Hawking	p174
86 Steve Jobs	p176
87 Sun Tzu	p178
88 Sylvia Plath	p180
89 Tennessee Williams	p182
90 Thomas Acquinas	p184
91 Thomas Edison	p186
92 Thomas Jefferson	p188
93 T.S. Eliot	p190
94 Vincent Van Gogh	p192
95 Virgil	p194
96 Voltaire	p195
97 Walt Disney	p197
98 William S. Burroughs	p199
99 William Shakespeare	p201
100 Winston Churchill	p202

1
Abraham Lincoln

1. Character is like a tree and reputation like a shadow. The shadow is what we think of it; the tree is the real thing.

2. You cannot escape the responsibility of tomorrow by evading it today.

3. The philosophy of the school room in one generation will be the philosophy of government in the next.

4. Don't worry when you are not recognized, but strive to be worthy of recognition.

5. Whatever you are, be a good one.

6. I'm a slow walker, but I never walk back.

7. No man has a good enough memory to be a successful liar.

8. Those who deny freedom to others deserve it not for themselves; and under the rule of a just God, cannot long retain it.

9. The things I want to know are in books; my best friend is the man who'll get me a book I ain't read.

10. The probability that we may fail in the struggle ought not to deter us from the support of a cause we believe to be just.

2
Aesop

11. The injuries we do and those we suffer are seldom weighed in the same scales.

12. He that always gives way to others will end in having no principles of his own.

13. A doubtful friend is worse than a certain enemy.

14. After all is said and done, more is said than done.

15. A crust eaten in peace is better than a banquet partaken in anxiety.

16. Better be wise by the misfortunes of others than by your own.

17. Beware lest you lose the substance by grasping the shadow.

18. Please all and you will please none.

19. Be content with your lot; one cannot be first in everything.

20. Our insignificant is often the cause of our safety.

3
Albert Einstein

21. Whoever is careless with the truth in small matters cannot be trusted with important matters.

22. The world is a dangerous place to live; not because of the people who are evil, but because of the people who don't do anything about it.

23. Logic will get you from A to B. Imagination will take you everywhere.

24. The only source of knowledge is experience.

25. Education is what remains after one has forgotten what one has learned in school.

26. It is the supreme art of the teacher to awaken joy in creative expression and knowledge.

27. Any man who can drive safely while kissing a pretty girl is simply not giving the kiss the attention it deserves.

28.   Once we accept our limits, we go beyond them.

29.   Reading, after a certain age, diverts the mind too much from its creative pursuits. Any man who reads too much and uses his own brain too little falls into lazy habits of thinking.

30.   Intellectual growth should commence at birth and cease only at death.

4
Aldous Huxley

31. Maybe this world is another planet's hell.

32. Experience is not what happens to you; it's what you do with what happens to you.

33. That men do not learn very much from the lessons of history is the most important of all the lessons of history.

34. Children are remarkable for their intelligence and ardor, for their curiosity, their intolerance of shams, the clarity and ruthlessness of their vision.

35. The most valuable of all education is the ability to make yourself do the thing you have to do, when it has to be done, whether you like it or not.

36. There are things known and there are things unknown, and in between are the doors of perception.

37. Beauty is worse than wine, it intoxicates both the holder and the beholder.

38. To travel is to discover that everyone is wrong about other countries.

39. Proverbs are always platitude until you have personally experienced the truth of them.

40. You shall know the truth and the truth shall make you mad.

5
Aristotle

41. My best friend is the man who in wishing me well wishes it for my sake.

42. It is the mark of an educated mind to be able to entertain a thought without accepting it.

43. We are what we repeatedly do. Excellence, then, is not an act, but a habit.

44. At his best, man is the noblest of all animals; separated from law and justice he is the worst.

45. The aim of the wise is not to secure pleasure but to avoid pain.

46. Pleasure in the job puts perfection in the work.

47. Good habits formed at youth make all the difference.

48. Wishing to be friends is quick work, but friendship is a slow ripening fruit.

49. For one swallow does not make a summer and so too one day does not make a man happy.

50. Courage is the first of human qualities because it is the quality which guarantees the others.

6
Arthur Conan Doyle

51. It is a capital mistake to theorize before one has data.

52. Any truth is better than indefinite doubt.

53. There is nothing more deceptive than an obvious fact.

54. My mind rebels at stagnation. Give me problems, give me work, give me the most abstruse cryptogram, or the most intricate analysis, and I am in my own proper atmosphere. But I abhor the dull routine of existence. I crave for mental exaltation.

55. Mediocrity knows nothing higher than itself, but talent instantly recognizes genius.

56. I have frequently gained my first real insight into the character of parents by studying their children.

57. Depend upon it there comes a time when for every addition of knowledge you forget something that you knew before. It is of the highest importance, therefore, not to

have useless facts elbowing out the useful ones.

58. For strange effects and extraordinary combinations we must go to life itself, which is always far more daring than any effort of the imagination.

59. A man should keep his little brain attic stocked with all the furniture that he is likely to sue, and the rest he can put away in the lumber room of his library, where he can get it if he wants.

60. To the man who loves art for its own sake, it is frequently in its least important and lowliest manifestations that the keenest pleasure is to be derived.

7
Arthur Miller

61. Maybe all one can do is hope to end up with the right regrets.

62. Betrayal is the only truth that sticks.

63. The theatre is so endlessly fascinating because it's so accidental. It's so much like life.

64. The apple cannot be stuck back on the Tree of Knowledge; once we begin to see, we are doomed and challenged to seek the strength to see more, not less.

65. Don't be seduced into thinking that which does not make a profit is without value.

66. If I can see an ending, I can work backward.

67. The closer a man approaches tragedy the more intense is his concentration of emotion upon the fixed point of his commitment, which is to say the closer he approaches what in life we call fanaticism.

68. I think it's a mistake to ever look for hope outside of one's self.

69. Everybody likes a kidder, but nobody lends him money.

70. All we are is a lot of talking nitrogen.

8
Benjamin Franklin

71. Tell me and I forget. Teach me and I remember. Involve me and I learn.

72. We are all born ignorant, but one must work hard to remain stupid.

73. An investment in knowledge pays the best interest.

74. Beware of little expenses. A small leak will sink a great ship.

75. Any fool can criticize, condemn and complain – and most fools do.

76. Whatever is begun in anger ends in shame.

77. Your net worth to the world is usually determined by what remains after your bad habits are subtracted from your good ones.

78. Life's Tragedy is that we get old too soon and wise too late.

79. You may delay but time will not.

80. How few there are who have courage enough to own their faults, or resolution enough to mend them.

9
Bruce Lee

81. Always be yourself, express yourself, have faith in yourself, do not go out and look for a successful personality and duplicate it.

82. Love is like a friendship caught on fire. In the beginning a flame, very pretty, often hot and flickering. As love grows older, our hearts mature and our love becomes as coals, deep-burning and unquenchable.

83. If you spend too much time thinking about a thing, you will never get it done.

84. I fear not the man who has practiced 10,000 kicks once, but I fear the man who has practiced one kick 10,000 times.

85. A goal is not always meant to be reached, it often serves simply as something to aim at.

86. To know oneself is to study oneself in action with another person.

87. If you love life, don't waste time, for time is what life is made up of.

88. A wise man can learn more from a foolish question than a fool can learn from a wise answer.

89. I'm not in this world to live up to your expectations and you're not in this world to live up to mine.

90. Notice that the stiffest tree is most easily cracked, while the bamboo or willow survives by bending with the wind.

10
Buddha

91. Health is the greatest gift, contentment the greatest wealth, faithfulness the best relationship.

92. You can search throughout the entire universe for someone who is more deserving of your love and affection than you are yourself, and that person is not to be found anywhere. You yourself, as much as anybody in the entire universe deserve your love and affection.

93. There are only two mistakes one can make along the road to truth; not going all the way and not starting.

94. Thousands of candles can be lighted from a single candle, and the life of the candle will not be shortened.

95. You will not be punished for your anger, you will be punished by your anger.

96. However many holy words you read, however many you speak, what good will they do you if you not act upon them?

97. Holding on to anger is like grasping a hot coal with the intent of throwing it at someone else; you are the one who gets burned.

98. It is better to travel well than to arrive.

99. A jug fills drop by drop.

100. What is the appropriate behavior for a man or a woman in the midst of this world, where each person is clinging to his piece of debris? What's the proper salutation between people as they pass each other in this flood?

11
Byron

101. There is pleasure in the pathless woods, there is rapture in the lonely shore, there is society where none intrudes, by the deep sea and music in its roar, I love not Man the less, but Nature more.

102. Be thou the rainbow in the storms of life.

103. The heart will break, but broken live on.

104. Laughter is the cheapest medicine.

105. Love will find a way through paths where wolves fear to prey.

106. Those who will not reason are bigots, those who cannot are fools, those who dare not are slaves.

107. Sorrow is knowledge, those that know the most must mourn the deepest, the tree of knowledge is not the tree of life.

108. Roll on, deep and dark blue ocean, roll. Ten thousand fleets sweep over thee in vain.

Man marks the Earth with ruin, but his control stops with the shore.

109. Death, so called, is a thing which makes men weep, and yet a third of life is passed in sleep.

110. The poor dog, in life the firmest friend. The first to welcome, foremost to defend.

12
Carl Jung

111. Everything that irritates us about others can lead us to an understanding of ourselves.

112. Even a happy life cannot be without a measure of darkness and the word happy would lose its meaning if it were not balanced by sadness.

113. We cannot change anything until we accept it.

114. Knowing your own darkness is the best method for dealing with the darknesses of other people.

115. Through pride, we are ever deceiving ourselves.

116. The shoe that fits one person pinches another; there is no recipe for living that suits all cases.

117. If there is anything that we wish to change in the child, we should first examine

it and see whether it is not something that could better be changed in ourselves.

118. The healthy man does not torture others – generally it is the tortured who turn into others.

119. The pendulum of the mind alternates between sense and nonsense, not between right and wrong.

120. A man who has not passed through the inferno of his passions has never overcome them.

13
Carl Sagan

121. Somewhere, something incredible is waiting to be known.

122. For me it is far better to grasp the universe as it really is than to persist in delusion however satisfying and reassuring.

123. Imagination will often carry us to worlds that never were. But without it, we go nowhere.

124. Extinction is the rule. Survival is the exception.

125. Absence of evidence is not evidence of absence.

126. For small creatures such as we, the vastness is bearable only through love.

127. The universe seems neither benign nor hostile, merely indifferent.

128. But the fact that some geniuses were laughed at does not imply that all who are laughed at are geniuses. They laughed at

Columbus, they laughed at the Wright Brothers. But they also laughed at Bozo the Clown.

129. Science is a way of thinking much more than it is a body of knowledge.

130. We live in a society exquisitely dependent on science and technology, in which hardly anyone knows anything about science and technology.

14
Chankaya

131. The fragrance of flowers spreads only in the direction of the wind. But goodness spreads in all directions.

132. Education is the best friend.

133. Before you start some work, always ask yourself three questions – Why am I doing it, what the results might be and Will I be successful.

134. A man is born alone and dies alone.

135. A man is great by deeds, not by birth.

136. A person should not be too honest. Straight trees are cut first and honest people are screwed first.

137. Never share your secrets with anybody. It will destroy you.

138. The serpent, the king, the tiger, the wasp, the small child, the dog owned by other people, and the fool; these seven ought not to be awakened from sleep.

139. There is poison in the fang of the serpent, in the mouth of the fly and in the sting of a scorpion, but the wicked man is saturated with it.

140. As a single withered tree, if set aflame, causes a whole forest to burn, so does a rascal son destroy a whole family.

15
Charles Bronte

141. The human heart has hidden treasures, In secret kept, in silence sealed; The thoughts, the hopes, the dreams, the pleasures, Whose charms were broken if revealed.

142. I am no bird; and no net ensnares me; I am a free human being with an independent will.

143. Life is so constructed, that the event does not, cannot, will not, match the expectation.

144. Give him enough rope and he will hang himself.

145. I try to avoid looking forward or backward, and try to keep looking upward.

146. Look twice before you leap.

147. If you are cast in a different mold to the majority, it is no merit of yours: Nature did it.

148. Better to be without logic than without feeling.

149. Men judge us by the success of our efforts. God looks at the efforts themselves.

150. It is vain to say human beings ought to be satisfied with tranquility; they must have action; and they will make it if they cannot find it.

16
Charles Darwin

151. A man who dares to waste one hour of time has not discovered the value of life.

152. An American monkey, after getting drunk on brandy, would never touch it again, and thus is much wiser than most men.

153. Ignorance more frequently begets confidence than does knowledge: it is those who know little, and not those who know much, who so positively assert that this or that problem will never be solved by science.

154. I love fool's experiments. I am always making them.

155. False facts are highly injurious to the progress of science, for they often endure long; but false views, if supported by some evidence, do little harm, for everyone takes a salutary pleasure in proving their falseness.

156. How paramount the future is to the present when one is surrounded by children.

157. A moral being is one who is capable of reflecting on his past actions and their motives – of approving of some and disapproving of others.

158. If the misery of the poor be caused not by the laws of nature, but by our institutions, great is our sin.

159. To kill an error is as good a service as, and sometimes even better than, the establishing of a new truth or fact.

160. It is a cursed evil to any man to become as adsorbed in any subject as I am in mine.

17
Charles Dickens

161. Have a heart that never hardens, and a temper that never tires, and a touch that never hurts.

162. The pain of parting is nothing to the joy of meeting again.

163. There are dark shadows on the earth, but its lights are stronger in the contrast.

164. No one is useless in this world who lightened the burden of it to anyone else.

165. It opens the lungs, washes the countenance, exercises the eyes, and softened down the temper; so cry away.

166. I will honor Christmas in my heart, and try to keep it all the year.

167. The whole difference between construction and creation is exactly this: that a thing constructed can only be loved after it is constructed: but a thing created is loved before it exists.

168. I can never close my lips where I have opened my heart.

169. A day wasted on others is not wasted on one's self.

170. Reflect upon your present blessings of which every man has many – not on your past misfortunes, of which all men have some.

18
Charlie Chaplin

171. A day without laughter is a day wasted.

172. To truly laugh, you must be able to take your pain and play with it.

173. Nothing is permanent, not even our troubles.

174. We think too much and feel too little.

175. Life is a tragedy when seen in close-up, but a comedy in long-shot.

176. I am at peace with God. My conflict is with Man.

177. Failure is unimportant.

178. It takes courage to make a fool of yourself.

179. I went into the business for the money, and the art grew out of it.

180. Man as an individual is a genius. But men in the mass form the headless monster,

a great, brutish idiot that goes where prodded.

19
Confucius

181. Life is really simple, but we insist on making it complicated.

182. Choose a job you love, and you will never have to work a day in your life.

183. When it is obvious that the goals cannot be reached, don't adjust the goals, adjust the action steps.

184. By three methods we may learn wisdom: First, by reflection, which noblest: Second, by imitation, which is easiest: and third by experience, which is the bitterest.

185. Real knowledge is to know the extent of one's ignorance.

186. If I am walking with two other men, each of them will serve as my teacher. I will out the good points of the one and imitate them, and the bad points of the other and correct them in myself.

187. The expectations of life depend upon diligence: the mechanic that would perfect his work must first sharpen his tools.

188. Never give a sword to a man who can't dance.

189. Better a diamond with a flaw than a pebble without.

190. He who learns but does not think is lost. He who thinks but does not learn is in great danger.

20
C.S. Lewis

191. You are never too old to set another goal.

192. It may be hard for an egg to turn into a bird: it would be a jolly sight harder for it to learn to fly while remaining an egg. We are like eggs at present. And you cannot go on indefinitely being just an ordinary, decent egg. We must be hatched or go bad.

193. Integrity is doing the right thing, even when no one is watching.

194. The task of the modern educator is not to cut down jungles, but to irrigate deserts.

195. Friendship has no survival value: rather it is one of those things that give value to survival.

196. Nothing that you have not given away will ever be really yours.

197. Literature adds to reality, it does not simply describe it.

198. Education without values, as useful as it is seems rather to make a man a more clever devil.

199. We all want progress, but if you're on the wrong road, progress means doing an about-turn and walking back to the right road: in that case, the man who turns back soonest is the most aggressive.

200. What we call Man's power over Nature turns out to be a power exercise by some men over other men with Nature as its instrument.

21
Dalai Lama

201. Happiness is not something ready made. It comes from your own actions.

202. Sleep is the best mediation.

203. In the practice of tolerance, one's enemy is the best teacher.

204. There is no need for temples, no need for complicated philosophies. My brain and my heart are my temples; my philosophy is kindness.

205. Technology really increased human ability. But technology cannot produce compassion.

206. We all have to live together so we might as well live together happily.

207. My desire to devolve authority has nothing to do with a wish to shirk responsibility.

208. I describe myself as a simple Buddhist monk. No more, no less.

209. If some people have the belief or view that the Dalai Lama has some miracle power, that's totally nonsense.

210. Of course, when I say that human nature is gentles, it is not 100 percent so. Every human being has that nature, but there are many people acting against their nature, being false.

22
Edgar Allen Poe

211. The boundaries which divide Life from Death are at best, shadowy and vague. Who shall say where the one ends, and where the other begins?

212. Words have no power to impress the mind without the exquisite horror of their reality.

213. The ninety and nine are with dreams, content but the hope of the world made anew, is the hundredth man who is grimly bent on making those dreams come true.

214. We loved with a love that was more than love.

215. Deep into that darkness peering, long I stood there, wondering, fearing, doubting, dreaming dreams no mortal ever dared to dream before.

216. Those who dream by day are cognizant of many things that escape those who dream only at night.

217. Beauty of whatever kind, in its supreme development, invariably excites the sensitive soul to tears.

218. I have great faith in fools; self-confidence my friends call it.

219. All that we see or seem is but a dream within a dream.

220. Experience has shown, and a true philosophy will always show, that a vast, perhaps the larger portion of the truth arises from the seemingly irrelevant.

23
Eleanor Roosevelt

221. With the new day comes new strength and new thoughts.

222. Great minds discuss ideas; average minds discuss events; small minds discuss people.

223. A woman is like a tea bad – you can't tell how strong she is until you put her in hot water.

224. We are afraid to care too much, for fear that the other person does not care at all.

225. Do things you think you cannot do.

226. Do what you feel in your to be right – for you'll be criticized anyway.

227. Never allow a person to tell you no who doesn't have the power to say yes.

228. It is not fair to ask of others what you are not willing to do yourself.

229. I think, at a child's birth, if a mother could ask a fairy godmother to endow it with the most useful gift, that gift should be curiosity.

230. I once had a rose named after me and I was very flattered. But I was not pleased to read the description in the catalogue: no good in a bed but fine up against a wall.

24
Emily Dickinson

231. I dwell in possibility.

232. Hope is the thing with feathers that perches in the soul – and sings the tunes without the words – and never stops at all.

233. If I can stop one heart from breaking, I shall not live in vain.

234. Behavior is what a man does, not what he thinks, feels, or believes.

235. Forever is composed of nows.

236. A wounded deer leaps the highest.

237. Where thou art, that is home.

238. How strange that nature does not knock, and yet does not intrude.

239. Dogs are better than human beings because they know but do not tell.

240. Old age comes on suddenly, and not gradually as is thought.

25
Ernest Hemingway

241. The best way to find out if you can trust somebody is to trust them.

242. The world breaks everyone, and afterward, some are strong at the broken places.

243. Never mistake motion for action.

244. Happiness in intelligent people is the rarest thing I know.

245. We are all apprentices in a craft where no one ever becomes a master.

246. The only good thing that could spoil a day was people. People were always the limiters of happiness except for the very few that were as good as spring itself.

247. They wrote in the old days that it is sweet and fitting to die for one's country. But in modern war, there is nothing sweet nor fitting in your dying. You will die like a god for no good reason.

248. Every man's life ends the same way. It is only the details of ho he lived and how he died that distinguish one man from another.

249. All things truly wicked start from innocence.

250. There is nothing to writing. All you do is sit down at a typewriter and bleed.

26
Euripides

251. Friends show their love in times of trouble, not in happiness.

252. One loyal friend is worth ten thousand relatives.

253. There is the sky which is all men's together.

254. Question everything. Learn something. Answer nothing.

255. Events will take their course, it is no good of being angry at them; he is happiest who wisely turns them to the best account.

256. Do not plan for ventures before finishing what's at hand.

257. Ten soldiers wisely led will beat a hundred without a head.

258. Talk sense to a fool and he calls you foolish.

259. The good and the wise lead quiet lives.

260. This is slavery, not to speak one's thought.

27
Francis Bacon

261. The best part of beauty is that which no picture can express.

262. In order for the light to shine so brightly, the darkness must be present.

263. Knowledge is power.

264. Age appears to be best in four things; old wood best to burn, old win to drink, old friends to trust, and old authors to read.

265. Silence is the sleep that nourishes wisdom.

266. I will never be an old man. To me, old age is always 15 years older than I am.

267. There is no comparison between that which is lost by not succeeding and that which is lost by not trying.

268. A bachelor's life is a fine breakfast, a flat lunch, and a miserable dinner.

269.   Reading maketh a full man; conference a ready man; and writing an exact man.

270.   The job of the artist is always to deepen the mystery.

28
Franz Kafka

271. By believing passionately in something still does not exist, we create it. The nonexistent is whatever we have not sufficiently desired.

272. Anyone who keeps the ability to see beauty never grows old.

273. I cannot force myself to use drugs to cheat on my loneliness.

274. The thornbush is the old obstacle in the road. It must catch fire if you want to go further.

275. A stair not worn hollow by footsteps is, regarded from its own point of view, only a boring something made of wood.

276. In argument, similes are like songs in love; they describe much, but prove nothing.

277. The spirit becomes free only when it ceases to be a support.

278. One tells as few lies as possible only by telling as few lies as possible, and not by having the least possible opportunity to do so.

279. A book must be the ax for the frozen sea within us.

280. Youth is happy because it has the ability to see beauty. Anyone who keeps the ability to see beauty never grows old.

29
Friedrich Nietzsche

281. We love life, not because we are used to living but because we are used to loving.

282. Whoever fights monsters should to it that in the process, he does not become a monster. And if you gaze long enough into an abyss, the abyss will gaze back into you.

283. The individual has always had to struggle to keep from being overwhelmed by the tribe. If you try it, you will be lonely often, and sometimes frightened. But no price is too high to pay for the privilege of owning yourself.

284. On the mountains of truth, you can never climb in vain; either you will reach a point higher up today, or you will be training your powers so that you will be able to climb higher tomorrow.

285. All things are subject to interpretation, whichever interpretation prevails at a given time is a function of power and not truth.

286. He who would learn to fly one day must first learn to stand and walk and run and climb and dance; one cannot fly into flying.

287. Thoughts are the shadows of our feelings – always darker, emptier and simpler.

288. To live is to suffer, to survive is to find some meaning in the suffering.

289. The love of power is the demon of men.

290. It is impossible to suffer without making someone pay for it; every complaint already contains revenge.

30
F. Scott Fitzgerald

291. Vitality shows in not only the ability to persist but the ability to start over.

292. Show me a hero and I'll write you a tragedy.

293. First you take a drink, then the drink takes a drink, then the drink takes you.

294. All good writing is swimming under water and holding your breath.

295. Forgotten is forgiven.

296. Personality is an unbroken series of successful gestures.

297. It is sadder to find the past again and find it inadequate to the present than it is to have it elude you and remain forever a harmonious conception of memory.

298. There are only the pursued, the pursuing, the busy and the tired.

299. My idea is always to reach my generation. The wise writer writes for the youth of his own generation, the critics of the next, and the schoolmasters of ever afterward.

300. Genius is the ability to put into effect what is on your mind.

31
Fyodor Dostoevsky

301. There are things which a man is afraid to tell even to himself, ad every decent man has a number of such things stored away in his mind.

302. Man is fond of counting his troubles, but he does not count his joys.

303. There is no subject so old that something new cannot be said about it.

304. The soul is healed by being with children.

305. Much unhappiness has come into the world because of bewilderment and things left unsaid.

306. Power is given only to those who dare to lower themselves and pick it up.

307. A real gentleman, even if he loses everything he owns, must show no emotion. Money must be so far beneath a gentleman that it is hardly worth troubling about.

308. To love someone means to see him as God intended him.

309. The greatest happiness is to know the source of unhappiness.

310. Happiness does not lie in happiness, but in the achievement of it.

32
Galileo Galilei

311. We cannot teach people anything; we can only help them discover it with themselves.

312. The sun, with all those planets revolving around it and dependent on it, can still ripen a bunch of grapes as if it had nothing else in the universe to do.

313. All truths are easy to understand once they are discovered; the point is to discover them.

314. I think that in the discussion of natural problems, we ought to begin not with the Scriptures, but with experiments and demonstrations.

315. I have never met a man so ignorant that I couldn't learn something from him.

316. Facts which at first seem improbably will, even on scant explanation, drop the cloak which has hidden them and stand forth in naked and simple beauty.

317. Where the senses fail us, reason must step in.

318. Measure what is measurable, and make measurable what is not so.

319. In questions of science, the authority of a thousand is not worth the humble reasoning of a single individual.

320. It is surely to souls to make heresy to believe what is proved.

33
George Bernard Shaw

321. Life is not about finding yourself. Life is about creating yourself.

322. We are made wise not by the recollection of our past, but by the responsibility for our future.

323. Beware of false knowledge; it is more dangerous than ignorance.

324. Progress is impossible without change, and those who cannot change their minds cannot change anything.

325. The single biggest problem in communication is the illusion that it has taken place.

326. Patriotism is your conviction that this country is superior to all others because you were born in it.

327. Do what must be done. This may not be happiness, but it is greatness.

328. A happy family is but an earlier heaven.

329. Success does not consist in never making mistakes but in never making the same one a second time.

330. Better keep yourself clean and bright; you are the window through which you must see the world.

34
George Orwell

331. Freedom is the right to tell people what they do not want to hear.

332. In a time of universal deceit – telling the truth is a revolutionary act.

333. Who controls the past controls the future. Who controls the present controls the past.

334. Men can only be happy when they do not assume that the object of life is happiness.

335. People sleep peaceably in their beds at night only because rough men stand ready to do violence on their behalf.

336. Each generation imagines itself to be more intelligent than the one that went before it, and wiser than the one that comes after it.

337. The essence of being human is that one does not seek perfection.

338. Myths which are believed in tend to become true.

339. Progress is not an illusion, it happens, but it is slow and invariably disappointing.

340. Power is not a means, it is an end.

35
George Santayana

341. The family is one of nature's masterpieces.

342. To be interested in the changing seasons is a happier state of mind than to be hopelessly in love with spring.

343. We must welcome the future, remembering that soon it will be the past; and we must respect the past, remembering that it was once all that was humanly possible.

344. Never build your emotional life on the weakness of others.

345. Wise men speak and fools decide.

346. It is a revenge the devil sometimes takes upon the virtuous, that he entraps them by the force of the very passion they have suppressed and think themselves superior to.

347. Only the dead have seen the end of war.

348. Wisdom comes by disillusionment.

349. Sanity is a madness put to good use.

350. A child educated only at school is an uneducated child.

36
George Washington

351. Liberty, when it begins to take root, is a plant of rapid growth.

352. Discipline is the soul of an army. It makes small numbers formidable.

353. True friendship is a plant of slow growth, and must undergo and withstand the shocks of adversity, before it is entitled to the appellation.

354. Labor to keep alive in your breast that little spark of celestial fire, called conscience.

355. Few men have virtue to withstand the highest bidder.

356. Be courteous to all, but intimate with few, and let those few be well tried before you give them your confidence.

357. Happiness and moral duty are inseparably connected.

358. Guard against the impostures of pretended patriotism.

359. When we assumed the Solider, we did not lay aside the Citizen.

360. Truth will ultimately prevail where there is pains to bring it to light.

37
Henry Ford

361. Coming together is a beginning; keeping together is progress; working together is success.

362. Thinking is the hardest work there is, which is probably the reason why so few engage in it.

363. My best friend is the one who brings out the best in me.

364. Don't find fault, find a remedy.

365. If money is your hope for independence you will never have it.

366. Life is a series of experiences, each one of which makes us bigger, even though sometimes it is hard to realize this.

367. This world was built to develop character.

368. We must learn that the setbacks and grieves which we endure help us in our marching onward.

369. Anyone who stops leaning is old, whether at twenty or eighty. Anyone who keeps learning stays young. The greatest thing in life is to keep your mind young.

370. If everyone is moving forward together, then success takes care of itself.

38
Henry Ibsen

371. A forest bird never wants a cage.

372. The spirit of truth and freedom – these are the pillars of society.

373. We are society's tools, neither more nor less.

374. The strongest man in the world is he who stand most alone.

375. People who don't know how to keep themselves healthy ought to have the decency to get themselves buried, and not waste time about it.

376. A community is like a ship; everyone ought to be prepared to take the helm.

377. The spectacles of experience through them you will see clearly a second time.

378. Home life ceases to be free and beautiful as soon as it is founded on borrowing and debt.

379. The majority is always wrong, the minority is rarely right.

380. It is inexcusable for scientists to torture animals; let them make their experiments on journalists and politicians.

39
H. G. Wells

381. If you feel down yesterday, stand up today.

382. Affliction comes to us, not to make us sad but sober; not to make us sorry but wise.

383. Beauty is in the heart of the beholder.

384. The path of the least resistance is the path of the loser.

385. Adapt or perish.

386. Our true nationality is mankind.

387. Heresies are experiments in man's unsatisfied search for truth.

388. If we don't end war, war will end us.

389. Human history becomes more and more a race between education and catastrophe.

390. Human history is the history of ideas.

40
Hippocrates

391. Cure sometimes, treat often, comfort always.

392. Healing is a matter of time, but it is sometimes also a matter of opportunity.

393. It is more important to know what sort of person has a disease than to know what sort of disease a person has.

394. Let food be thy medicine and medicine be thy food.

395. Natural forces within us are the true healers of disease.

396. Many admire, few know.

397. Life is short, the art long.

398. Everything in excess is opposed to nature.

399. There are in fact two things, science and opinion; the former begets knowledge, the later ignorance.

400. The chief virtue that language can have is clearness, and nothing detracts from it so much as the use of unfamiliar words.

41
Homer

401. There is nothing nobler or more admirable than when two people who see eye to eye keep house as man and wife, confounding their enemies and delighting their friends.

402. And what he greatly thought, he nobly dared.

403. The difficulty is not so great to die for a friend, as to find a friend worth dying for.

404. Yet, taught by tie, my heart has learned to glow for other's good and melt at other's woe.

405. The charity that is trifle to us can be precious to others.

406. It is not good to have a rule of many.

407. But curb thou the high spirit in thy breast, for gentle ways are best, and keep aloof from sharp contentions.

408. In youth and beauty, wisdom is but rare.

409. A decent boldness ever meets with friends.

410. Two urns on Jove's high throne has ever stood, the source of evil one, and one of good; from thence the cup of mortal man he fills, blessings to these, to those distributes ills, to most he mingles both.

42
Honor de Balzac

411. A woman knows the face of the man she loves as a sailor knows the open sea.

412. A mother's happiness is like a beacon, lighting up the future but reflected also on the past in the guise of fond memories.

413. There is no such thing as a great talent without great willpower.

414. Love is the poetry of the senses.

415. It is easy to sit up and take notice, what is difficult is getting up and taking action.

416. Power is not revealed by striking hard or often, but by striking true.

417. Those who spend too fast never grow rich.

418. Thought is the key to all treasures.

419. Art is nature concentrated.

420. Conscience is our unerring judge until we finally stifle it.

43
Isaac Asimov

421. Science gathers knowledge faster than society gathers wisdom.

422. The true delight is in the finding out rather than in the knowing.

423. No sensible decision can be made any longer without taking account not only the world as it is, but the world as it will be.

424. Life is pleasant. Death is peaceful. It's the transition that's troublesome.

425. Writing, to me, is simply thinking through my fingers.

426. A subtle thought that is in error may yet give rise to fruitful inquiry that can establish truths of great value.

427. I am not a speed reader. I am speed understander.

428. Violence is the last refuge of the incompetent.

429. It is not only the living who are killed in war.

430. Self-education is, I firmly believe, the only kind of education there is.

44
Isaac Newton

431. We build too many walls and not enough bridges.

432. I do not know what I may appear to the world, but to myself I seem to have been only like a boy playing on the seashore, and diverting myself in now and then finding a smoother pebble or a prettier shell than ordinary, whilst the great ocean of truth all undiscovered before me.

433. I can calculate the motion of heavenly bodies, but not the madness of people.

434. Tact is the art of making a point without making an enemy.

435. Truth is ever to be found in simplicity, and not in the multiplicity and confusion of things.

436. Genius is patience.

437. My powers are ordinary. Only my application brings me success.

438. What goes up must come down.

439. It is the weight, not numbers of experiments that is to be regarded.

440. Plato is my friend; Aristotle is my friend, but my greatest friend is truth.

45
James Joyce

441. Mistakes are the portals of discovery.

442. I am tomorrow what I am establish today.

443. My mouth is full of decayed teeth and my soul of decayed ambitions.

444. Better pass boldly into that other world, in the full glory of some passion, than fade and wither dismally with age.

445. Think you're escaping and run into yourself.

446. Longest way round is the shortest way home.

447. Your battles inspired me – not the obvious battles but those that were fought and won behind your forehead.

448. The actions of men are the best interpreters of their thoughts.

449. I've put in so many enigmas and puzzles that it will keep the professors busy for centuries arguing over what I meant, and that's the only way of insuring one's immortality.

450. He found in the world without as actual what was in his world within as possible.

46
Jane Austen

451. Vanity and pride are different things, though the words are often used synonymously. Pride relates more to our opinion of ourselves; vanity, to what we would have others think of us.

452. Selfishness must always be forgiven, because there is no hope of a cure.

453. There are people, who the more you do for them, the less they will do for themselves.

454. Happiness in marriage is entirely a matter of chance.

455. One man's style must not be the rule of another's.

456. What is right cannot be done too soon.

457. How quick come the reasons for approving what we like.

458. Nobody minds having what is too good for them.

459. They are much to be pitied who have not been given a taste for nature early in life.

460. Those who do not complain are never pitied.

47
Jesus Christ

461. Love your enemies and pray for those who persecute you.

462. Ask and it will be given, search and you will find, knock and the door will open.

463. If you love those who love, what credit is that to you? For even sinners love those who love them. And if you do good to those who do good to you, what credit is that to you? For even sinners do the same.

464. If you want to be perfect, go, sell your possessions and give to the poor, and you will have treasure in heaven.

465. Let the one among you who is without sin be the first to cast a stone.

466. What you do not bring forth will destroy you.

467. It is not the healthy who need a doctor, but the sick. I have not come to call the righteous, but sinners to repentance.

468. Do not let your hearts be troubled. Trust in God, trust in me.

469. As I have loved you, so you must love one another.

470. Know that I am with you always, yes, to the end of time.

48
John F. Kennedy

471. As we express our gratitude, we must never forget that the highest appreciation is not to utter words, but to live by them.

472. Change is the law of life.

473. Things do not happen. Things are made to happen.

474. Leadership and learning are indispensable to each other.

475. Efforts and courage are not enough without purpose and direction.

476. The best road to progress is freedom's road.

477. We are tied to the ocean. And when we go back to the sea, whether it is to sail or to watch – we are going back from whence we came.

478. The goal of education is the advancement of knowledge and the dissemination of truth.

479. A man may die, nations may rise and fall, but an idea lives on.

480. The cost of freedom is always high.

49
John Lennon

481. Love is a flower, you've got to let it grow.

482. We've got this gift of love, but love is like a precious plant. You can't just accept it and leave it in the cupboard or just think it's going to get on by itself. You've got to keep watering it. You've got to really look after it and nurture it.

483. When you're drowning, you don't say, "I would be incredibly pleased if someone would have the foresight to notice me drowning and come and help me." You just scream.

484. Imagine all the people living life in peace. You may say I'm a dreamer, but I'm not the only one. I hope someday you'll join us, and the world will be as one.

485. Everything is clearer when you're in love.

486. Reality leaves a lot to the imagination.

487. I believe in everything until it's disproved.

488. Everybody loves you when you're six foot in the ground.

489. Give peace a chance.

490. The more I see, the less I know for sure.

50
John Milton

491. Gratitude bestows reverence, allowing us to encounter everyday epiphanies, those transcendent moments of awe that change forever how we experience life and the world.

492. They also serve who only stand and wait.

493. He that has light within his own clear breast, May sit in the center, and enjoys bright day; But he that hides a dark soul and foul thoughts, Benighted walks under the midday sun; Himself his own dungeon.

494. Death is the golden key that opens the palace of eternity.

495. Beauty is nature's brag.

496. The mind is its own place and in itself, can make a Heaven of Hell, a Hell of Heaven.

497. The superior man acquaints himself with many sayings of antiquity and many

deeds of the past, in order to strengthen his character thereby.

498. The stars, that nature hung in heaven, and filled their lamps with everlasting oil, give due light to the mislead and lonely traveler.

499. Who kills a man, kills a reasonable creature, God's image, but thee who destroy a good book, kill reason its self.

500. But what can war, but endless war, still breed?

51
John Steinbeck

501. I have come to believe that a great teacher is a great artist and that there are as few as there are any other greatest artists. Teaching might even be the greatest of the arts since the medium is the human mind and spirit.

502. It is a common experience that a problem difficult at night is resolved in the morning after the committee of sleep has worked on it.

503. A journey is a person in itself; no two are alike.

504. We do not take a trip, a trip takes us.

505. You only want advice if it agrees with you.

506. A sad soul can kill quicker than a germ.

507. One can find so many pains when the rain is falling.

508. If you're in trouble, or hurt or need – go to the poor people. They're the only ones that'll help – the only ones.

509. Many a trip continues long after movement in time and space have ceased.

510. The writer must believe that what he is doing is the most important thing in the world. And he must hold to this illusion even when he knows it is not true.

52
Jonathan Swift

511. Vision is the art of seeing what is invisible to others.

512. A wise man should have money in his head, but not in his heart.

513. May all you live all the days of your life.

514. The proper words in the proper places are the true definition of style.

515. When a true genius appears, you can know him by this sign; that all the dunces are in a confederacy against him.

516. Books, the children of the brain.

517. For in reason, all government without the consent of the governed is the very definition of slavery.

518. The power of fortune is confessed only by the miserable, for the happy impute all their success to prudence or merit.

519. A lie does not consist in the indirect position of words, but in the desire and intention, by false speaking, to deceive and injure your neighbor.

520. One enemy can do more hurt than ten friends can do good.

53
Joseph Campbell

521. Find a place inside where there's joy, and the joy will burn out the pain.

522. The privilege of a lifetime is being who you are.

523. Your sacred space is where you can find yourself again and again.

524. We must let go of the life we have planned, so as to accept the one that is waiting for us.

525. When we quit thinking primary about ourselves and our own self-preservation, we undergo a truly heroic transformation of consciousness.

526. When you make the sacrifice in marriage, you're sacrificing not to each other but to unity in a relationship.

527. I don't believe people are looking for the meaning of life as much as they are looking for the experience of being alive.

528. Your life is the fruit of your own doing. You have no one to blame but yourself.

529. The goal of life is to make your heartbeat match the beat of the universe, to match your nature with Nature.

530. It is by going down into the abyss that we recover the treasure of life. Where you stumble, there lies your treasure.

54
Joseph Conrad

531. Who knows what true loneliness is – not the convention word but the naked terror? To the lonely themselves it wears a mask. The most miserable outcast hugs some memory or some illusion.

532. Being a woman is a terribly difficult task, since it consists principally in dealing with men.

533. I take it that what all men are really after is some formula of peace.

534. Great achievements are accomplished in a bless, warm fog.

535. History repeats itself, but the special call of an art which has passed away is never reproduced. It is as utterly gone out of the world as the song of a destroyed wild bird.

536. In order to move other deeply we must deliberately allow ourselves to be carried away beyond the bounds of our normal sensibility.

537. Face it, that's the way to get through.

538. Gossip is what no one claims to like, but everybody enjoys.

539. Woe to the man whose heart has not learned while young to hope, to love – and to put its trust in life.

540. A caricature is putting the face of a joke on the body of a truth.

55
Jules Verne

541. Imagine a society in which there were neither rich nor poor. What evils, afflictions, sorrows, disorders, catastrophes, disasters, tribulations, misfortunes, agonies, calamities, despair, desolation and ruin would be unknown to man.

542. In spite of the opinions of certain narrow-minded people, who would shut up the human race upon this globe, as within some magic circle it must never outstep, we shall one day travel to the moon, the planet, and the stars, with the same facility, rapidity, and certainty as we now make the voyage from Liverpool to New York.

543. However strong, however imposing a ship may appear, it is not disgraced because it flies before the tempest. A commander ought always to remember that a man's life is worth more than the mere satisfaction of his own pride. In any case, to be obstinate is blamable, and to be wilful is dangerous.

544. We may brave human laws, but we cannot resist natural ones.

545. Science is made up of mistakes, but they are mistakes which it is useful to make, because they lead little by little to the truth.

546. Solitude is beyond human endurance.

547. You're never rich enough if you can be richer.

548. Trains, like time and tide, stop for no one.

549. Put two ships in the open sea, without wind or tide, and, at last, they will come together. Throw two planets into space, and they will fall one on the other. Place two enemies in the midst of a crowd, and they will inevitably meet; it is a fatality, a question of time; that is all.

550. Liberty is worth paying for.

56
Julius Caesar

551. Experience is the teacher of all things.

552. It is easier to find men who will volunteer to die, than to find those who are willing to endure pain with patience.

553. No one is so brave that he is not disturbed by something unexpected.

554. It is better to create than to learn.

555. What we wish, we readily believe, and what we ourselves think, we imagine others think also.

556. Men worry more about what they can't see than about what they can.

557. Men are quick to believe that which they wish to be true.

558. I rather be first in a village than second at Rome.

559. I love the name of honor, more than I fear death.

560. I came, I saw, I conquered.

57
Leo Tolstoy

561. Everyone thinks of changing the world, but no one thinks of changing himself.

562. The two most powerful warriors are patience and time.

563. If you want to be happy, be.

564. There is no greatness where there is no simplicity, goodness and truth.

565. I sit on a man's back, choking him and making him carry me, and yet assure myself and others that I am very sorry for him and wish to ease his lot by all possible means – except by getting off his back.

566. Joy can only be real if people look upon their life as a service and have a definite object in life outside themselves and their personal happiness.

567. All violence consists in some people forcing others, under threat of suffering or death, to do what they do not want to do.

568. The changes in our life must come from the impossibility to live otherwise than according to the demands of our conscience not from our mental resolution to try a new form of life.

569. Art is not a handicraft, it is the transmission of feeling the artist has experienced.

570. Music is the shorthand of emotion.

58
Lewis Carroll

571. If you don't know where you are going, any road will get you there.

572. I can't go back to yesterday because I was a different person then.

573. Who in the world am I? Ah, that's the great puzzle.

574. Sometimes I've believed as many as six impossible things before breakfast.

575. She generally gave herself very good advice (thought she very seldom followed it.)

576. While the laughter of joy is in full harmony with our deeper life, the laughter of amusement should be kept apart from it. The danger is too great of thus learning to look at solemn things in a spirit of mockery, and to seek in them opportunities for exercising wit.

577. Contrariwise, if it was so, it might be; and if it were so, it would be; but as it isn't, it ain't. That's logic.

578. That's the reason they're called lessons, because they lesson from day to day.

579. All that is really worth the doing is what we do for others.

580. Everything's got a moral, if only you can find it.

59
Ludwig von Beethoven

581. Music is a higher revelation than all wisdom and philosophy.

582. Music is the mediator between the spiritual and the sensual life.

583. Music should strike fire from the heart of man, and bring tears from the eyes of woman.

584. Tones sound, and roar and storm about me until I have set them down in notes.

585. A great poet is the most precious jewel of a nation.

586. Don't only practice your art, but force your way into its secrets; art deserves that, for it and knowledge can raise man to the Divine.

587. Art, who comprehends her? With whom can one consult concerning this great goddess?

588. What you are, you are by accident of birth; what I am, I am by myself. There are and will be a thousand princes; there is only one Beethoven.

589. Recommend virtue to your children; it alone, not money, can make them happy. I speak from experience.

590. Music is the one incorporeal entrance into the higher world of knowledge which comprehends mankind but which mankind cannot comprehend.

60
Mahatma Gandhi

591. Happiness is when what you think, what you say, and what you do are in harmony.

592. Only the weak never forgive.

593. The best way to find yourself is to lose yourself in the service of others.

594. Humanity is an ocean; if a few drops of the ocean are dirty, the ocean does not become dirty.

595. Prayer is the key of the morning and the bolt of the evening.

596. Non-force is the greatest force at the disposal of mankind.

597. Action expresses priorities.

598. What difference does it make to the dead, the orphans, and the homeless, whether the mad destruction is wrought under the name of totalitarianism or the holy name of liberty or democracy?

599. The moment there is suspicion about a person's motives, everything he does becomes tainted.

600. Honest disagreement is often a good sign of progress.

61
Marcus Aurelius

601. Everything we hear is an opinion, not a fact.

602. The art of living is more like wrestling than dancing.

603. Within is the fountain of good, and it will ever bubble up, if thou wilt ever dig.

604. The best revenge is to be unlike him who performed the injury.

605. The soul becomes dyed with the color of its thoughts.

606. Confine yourself to the present.

607. It is not death that a man should fear, but he should fear never beginning to live.

608. Everything that happens happens as it should, and if you observe carefully, you will find this to be so.

609. A man's worth is no greater than his ambitions.

610. Each day provides its own gifts.

62
Mark Twain

611. The secret of getting ahead is getting started.

612. Whenever you find yourself on the side of the majority, it is time to pause and reflect.

613. A man who lives fully is prepared to die any time.

614. Anger is an acid that can do more harm to the vessel in which it is stored than to anything on which it is poured.

615. You can't depend on your eyes when your imagination is out of focus.

616. Do the right thing. It will gratify some people and astonish the rest.

617. Many a small thing has been made large by the right kind of advertising.

618. Don't go around saying the world owes you a living. The world owes you nothing. It was here first.

619. When in doubt, tell the truth.

620. It ain't what you don't know that gets you into trouble. It's what you know for sure that just ain't so.

63
Martin Luther King

621. The ultimate measure of a man is not where he stands in moments of comfort and convenience, but where he stands at time of challenge and controversy.

622. There is some good in the worst of us and some evil in the best of us.

623. In the End, we will remember not the words of our enemies, but the silence of our friends.

624. A man can't ride you unless your back is bent.

625. Change does not roll in on the wheels of inevitability, but comes through continuous struggle.

626. I refuse to accept the view that mankind is so tragically bound to the starless midnight of racism and war that the bright daybreak of peace and brotherhood can never become a reality... I believe that unarmed truth and unconditional love will have the final word.

627. A genuine leader is not a searcher for consensus but a molder of consensus.

628. We may have all come on different ships, but we're in the same boat now.

629. Nothing pains some people more than having to think.

630. Injustice anywhere is a threat to justice everywhere.

64
Maya Angelou

631. Try to be a rainbow in someone's cloud.

632. I've learned that people will forget what you said, people will forget what you did, but people will never forget how you made them feel.

633. My mother said I must always be intolerant of ignorance but understanding of illiteracy. That some people, unable to go school, were more educated and more intelligent than college professors.

634. Nothing will work unless you do.

635. You may not control all the events that happen to you, but you decide not to be reduced by them.

636. Love recognize no barriers. It jumps hurdles, leap fences, penetrates walls to arrive at its destination full of hope.

637. History cannot be unlived.

638. Bitter is like cancer, it eats upon the host.

639. All great achievements require time.

640. A wise woman wishes to be no one's enemy; a wise woman refuses to be anyone's victim.

65
Michio Kaku

641. What we usually consider as impossible are simply engineering problems... there's no law of physics preventing them.

642. Boring exams is the well from which we draw our nourishment and energy.

643. The human brain has 100 billion neurons, each neuron connected to 10,000 other neurons. Sitting om your shoulders is the most complicated object in the known universe.

644. It's pointless to have a nice clean desk, because it means you're not doing anything.

645. If a Martian came down to Earth and watched television, he'd come to conclusion that all world's society is based on Britney Spears and Paris Hilton. He'd be amazed that our society hasn't collapsed.

646. Our grandkids will lead the lives of the gods of mythology. Zeus could think and move objects around. We'll have that power. Venus had a perfect, timeless body. We'll

have that, too. Pegasus was a flying horse. We'll be able to modify life in the future.

647. We have to realize that science is a double-edged sword. One edge of the sword can cut against poverty, illness, disease and give us more democracies, and democracies never war with other democracies, but the other side of the sword could give us nuclear proliferation, biogerms and even forces of darkness.

648. The word "impossible" is dangerous.

649. Nothing is ever 100% proven.

650. You can mass-produce hardware; you cannot mass-produce software – you cannot mass-produce the human mind.

66
Moliere

651. A wise man is superior to any insults which can be put upon him and the best reply to unseemly behavior is patience and moderation.

652. The trees that are slow to grow bear the best fruit.

653. People don't mind being mean; but they never want to be ridiculous.

654. Speak to be understood.

655. I live on soup, not on fine words.

656. I prefer a pleasant vice to an annoying virtue.

657. It is not only for what we do that we are held responsible, but also for what we do not do.

658. It infuriates me to be wrong when I know when I'm right.

659. A learned fool is more than an ignorant fool.

660. If you suppress grief too much, it can well redouble.

67
Muhammad Ali

661. Friendship is not something you learn in school. But if you haven't learned the meaning of friendship, you really haven't learned anything.

662. I hated every minute of training, but I said, "Don't quit. Suffer now and live the rest of your life as a champion."

663. Silence is golden when you can't think of a good answer.

664. Service to others is the rent you pay for your room here on Earth.

665. The fight is won or lost far away from the witnesses – behind the lies in the gym, and out there on the road, long before I dance under those lights.

666. Only a man who knows what it is like to be defeated can reach down to the bottom of his soul and come up with the extra ounce of power it takes to win when the match is even.

667. What keeps me going is goals.

668. Rivers, ponds, lakes and streams – they all have different names, but they all contain water. Just as religions do – they all contain truths.

669. It's not bragging if you can back it up.

670. I had been so great in boxing, they had to create an image like Rocky, a white image on the screen, to counteract my image in the ring. America has to have its white images, no matter it gets them. Jesus, Wonder Woman, Tarzan and Rocky.

68
Napoleon Bonaparte

671. History is the version of past events that people have decided to agree upon.

672. Impossible is a word to be found only in the dictionary of fools.

673. Death is nothing, but to live defeated and inglorious is to die daily.

674. A solider will fight long and hard for a bit of colored ribbon.

675. Victory belongs to the most persevering.

676. Take time to deliberate, but when the time for action has arrived, stop thinking and go in.

677. You must not fight too often with one enemy, or you will teach him all your art of war.

678. Ten people who speak make more noise than ten thousand who are silent.

679. There is no such thing as accident; it is fate misnamed.

680. I am sometimes a fox and sometimes a lion. The whole secret of government lies in knowing when to be the one or the other.

69 Neil deGrasse Tyson

681. What adults primarily do in the presence of kids is unwittingly thwart the curiosity of children.

682. Not enough people in this world, I think, carry a cosmic perspective with them. It could be life-changing.

683. Adults, who outnumber kids four or five to one, are in charge. We wield the resources, run the world, and completely thwart kids' creativity.

684. Everyone should have their mind blown once a day.

685. The history of exploration has never been driven by exploration. But Columbus himself was a discoverer. So was Magellan. But the people who wrote checks were not. They had other motivations.

686. Science is basically an inoculation against charlatans.

687. Space only becomes ordinary when the frontier is no longer being breached.

688. People who are scientists today are scientists in spite of the system, typically, not because of it.

689. I'm on a crusade to get movie directors to get their science right because, more often than they believe, the science is more extraordinary than anything they can invent.

690. One of the greatest features of science is that it doesn't matter where you were born, and it doesn't matter what the beliefs systems of your parents might have been; if you perform the same experiment that someone else did, at a different time and place, you'll get the same result.

70 Oscar Wilde

691. Keep love in your heart. A life without it is like a sunless garden when the flowers are dead.

692. Experience is simply the name we give our mistakes.

693. Women are made to be loved, not understood.

694. The old believe everything, the middle-aged suspect everything, the young know everything.

695. No great artists ever sees things as they really are. If he did, he would cease to be an artist.

696. Laughter is not at all a bad beginning for a friendship, and it is by far the best ending for one.

697. Some cause happiness wherever they go; others whenever they go.

698. All women become like their mothers. That is their tragedy. No man does. That's his.

699. Give a man a mask and he will the truth.

700. Consistency is the last refuge of the unimaginative.

71 Ovid

701. Beauty is a fragile gift.

702. The sharp thorn often produces delicate roses.

703. Habits change into character.

704. The man who has experienced shipwreck shudders even at a calm sea.

705. Men do not value a good deed unless it brings a reward.

706. We are ever striving after what is forbidden.

707. Make the workmanship surpass the materials.

708. In our leisure we reveal what kind of people we are.

709. You can learn from anyone, even your enemy.

710. What is without periods of rest will not endure.

72 Plato

711. You can discover more about a person in an hour of play than in a year of conversation.

712. Courage is knowing what not to fear.

713. Good people do not need laws to tell them to act responsibly, while bad people will find a way around the laws.

714. The measure of a man is what he does with power.

715. There are two things a person should be angry at, what they can help, and what they cannot.

716. He who is not a good servant will not be a good master.

717. One cannot practice many arts with success.

718. Thinking: the talking of the soul with itself.

719. There is no harm in repeating good deeds.

720. Poetry is nearer to vital truth than history.

73 Plautus

721. The greatest talents often lie buried out of sight.

722. Patience is the best remedy for every trouble.

723. A mouse does not rely on just one hole.

724. The day, water, sun, moon, night – I do not have to purchase these things with money.

725. Nothing is more wretched than the mind of a man conscious of guilt.

726. Keep what you have; the known evil is best.

727. Good courage in a bad affair is half of the evil overcome.

728. It is well for one to know more than he says.

729. You must spend money to make money.

730. He means well is useless unless he does well.

74 Pliny the Elder

731. The only certainty is that nothing is certain.

732. An object in possession seldom retains the same charm that it had in pursuit.

733. We grieve only for what we know has happened, but we fear all that possibly may happen.

734. We cannot be wise at all moments.

735. Home is where the heart is.

736. Truth comes out in wine.

737. From the end spring new beginnings.

738. The depth of darkness to which you can descend and still live is an exact measure of the height to which you can aspire to reach.

739. Wealth possess mankind rather than mankind possesses wealth.

740. It is generally much more shameful to lose a good reputation than never to have acquired it.

75
Ralph Waldo Emerson

741. To be yourself in a world that is constantly trying to make you something else is the greatest accomplishment.

742. For everything you have missed, you have gained something else, and for everything you gain, you lose something else.

743. Nothing great was ever achieved without enthusiasm.

744. Shallow men believe in luck. Strong men believe in cause and effect.

745. We gain the strength of the temptation we resist.

746. Age doesn't mean a thing. The best tunes are played on the oldest fiddles.

747. The reward of a thing well done is having done it.

748. Win as if you were used to it, lose as if you enjoyed it for a change.

749. Aim above the mark to hit the mark.

750. Knowledge is knowing that we cannot know.

76
Rene Descartes

751. If you would be a real seeker after truth, it is necessary that at least once in your life, you doubt all things, as far as possible.

752. Whenever anyone has offended me, I try to raise my soul so high that the offense cannot reach it.

753. The first precept was never to accept a thing as true until in knew it as such without a single doubt.

754. One cannot conceive anything so strange and so implausible that is has not already been said by one philosopher.

755. Each problem that I solved became a rule, which served afterwards to solve other problems.

756. There is nothing so strange and so unbelievable that it has not been said by one philosopher or another.

757. Illusory joy is often worth more than genuine sorrow.

758. I hope that posterity will judge me kindly, not only at to the things which I have explained, but also to those which I have intentionally omitted so as to leave to others the pleasure of discovery.

759. Everything is self-evident.

760. The two operations of our understanding, intuition and education, on which alone we have said we must rely in the acquisition of knowledge.

77
Richard Dawkins

761. Let's be open-minded, but not so open-minded that our brains drop out.

762. Teachers who help to open young minds perform a duty which is as near sacred as I will admit.

763. Metaphors are fine if they aid understanding, but sometimes they get in the way.

764. The universe doesn't owe us condolence or consolation; it doesn't owe us a nice warm feeling inside.

765. I accept that there may be things far grander and more incomprehensible than we can possibly imagine.

766. Words raise consciousness.

767. Hoe can you take seriously someone who likes to believe something because he finds it "comforting?"

768. The solution often turns out more beautiful than the puzzle.

769. Never be satisfied with not understanding the world.

770. A delusion is something people believe in desire a total lack of evidence.

78
Robert Lewis Stevenson

771. Don't judge each day by the harvest you reap but by the seeds that you plant.

772. A friend is a gift you give yourself.

773. Compromise is the cheapest lawyer.

774. I travel not to go anywhere, but to go.

775. Life is not a matter of holding good cards, but of playing a poor hand well.

776. Our life is not to succeed, but to continue to fail in good spirits.

777. Everybody, soon or late, sits down to a banquet of consequences.

778. The cruelest lies are often told in silence.

779. Keep your fears to yourself, but share your courage with others.

780. The Devil, can sometimes do a very gentlemanly thing.

79
Salvador Dali

781. Intelligence without ambition is a bird without wings.

782. Drawing is the honesty of the art. There is no possibility of cheating. It is either good or bad.

783. Have no fear of perfection – you'll never reach it.

784. I don't do drugs. I am drugs.

785. There is only one difference between a madman and me. The madman thinks he is sane. I know I am mad.

786. What is a television apparatus to man, who has only to shut his eyes to see the most inaccessible regions of the seen and the never seen.

787. The difference between false memories and true ones is the same as for jewels; it is always the false ones that look the most real.

788. Surrealism is destructive, but it destroys only what it considers to be shackles limiting our vision.

789. Money is a glory.

790. Don't bother to be modern.

80
Samuel Beckett

791. We are all born mad. Some remain so.

792. You're on Earth. There is no cure for that.

793. Words are all we have.

794. To find a form that accommodates the mess, that is the task of the artist now.

795. What do I know of man's destiny? I could tell you more about radishes.

796. The tears of the world are a constant quality. For each one who begins to weep, somewhere else another stops. The same is true of the laugh.

797. It is right that he too should have his little chronicle, his memories, his reason, and be able to recognize the good in the bad, the bad in the worst, and so grow gently old down all unchanging days, and die one day like any other day, only shorter.

798. Habit is a great deadener.

799. Poets are the sense, philosophers the intelligence of humanity.

800. Every word is like an unnecessary stain on silence and nothingness.

81
Sigmund Freud

801. Everywhere I go I find that a poet has been there before me.

802. He that has eyes to see and ears to hear may convince himself that no mortal can keep a secret. If his lips are silent, he chatters with his fingertips; betrayal oozes out of him at every pore.

803. The conscious mind may be compared to a fountain playing in the sun and falling back into the great subterranean pool of subconscious from which it rises.

804. Analysis does not set out to make pathological reactions impossible, but to give the patient' ego freedom to decide one way or another.

805. A man should not strive to eliminate his complexes but to get into accord with them; they are legitimately what what directs his conduct in the world.

806. If youth knew; if age could.

807. Most people do not really want freedom, because freedom involves responsibility, and most people are frightened of responsibility.

808. Love and work are the cornerstones of our humanness.

809. Illusions commend themselves to us because they save us pain and allows us to enjoy pleasure instead. We must therefore accept it without complaint when they sometimes collide with a bit of reality against which they are dashed to pieces.

810. He does not believe that does not live according to his belief.

82
Socrates

811. Beware the barrenness of a busy life.

812. If you get a good wife, you'll become happy; if you get a bad one, you'll become a philosopher.

813. Be as you wish to seem.

814. Wisdom begins in wonder.

815. True wisdom comes to each of us when we realize how little we understand about life, ourselves and the world around us.

816. Worthless people live only to eat and drink; people of worth eat and drink only to live.

817. Let him that would move the world, first move himself.

818. The unexamined life is not worth living.

819. An honest man is always a child.

820. If a man is proud of his wealth, he should not be praised until it is known how he employs it.

83
Sophocles

821. Who seeks shall find.

822. Rather fail with honor than succeed by fraud.

823. Trust dies, but mistrust blossoms.

824. If you were to offer a thirsty man all wisdom, you would not please him more than if you gave him a drink.

825. Children are the anchors that hold mother to life.

826. Quick decisions are unsafe decisions.

827. Success is dependent on effort.

828. Men should pledge themselves to nothing; for reflection makes a liar to their resolution.

829. No speech can stain what is noble by nature.

830. Old age and the passage of time teach all things.

84
Stephen Fry

831. Taste every fruit of every tree in the garden at least once. It is an insult to creation not to experience it fully. Temperance is wickedness.

832. You can't reason yourself back into cheerfulness any more than you can reason yourself into an extra six inches in height.

833. We admire what we are not.

834. I think we have all experienced passion that is not in any sense reasonable.

835. Having great intellect is no path to being happy.

836. I am a lover of truth, a worshipper of freedom, a celebrant at the altar of language and purity and tolerance.

837. Incuriosity is the oddest and most foolish failing there is.

838. One technology doesn't replace another, it complements. Books are no more

threatened by Kindle than stairs by elevators.

839. Life, that can shower you with so much splendor, is unremittingly cruel to those who have given up.

840. There is nothing so self-righteous nor so right as an adolescent imagination.

85
Stephen Hawking

841. In my opinion, there is no aspect of reality beyond the reach of the human mind.

842. No one undertakes research in physics with the intention of wining a prize. It is the joy of discovering something no one knew before.

843. Scientists have become the bearers of the torch of discovery in our quest for knowledge.

844. My goal is simple. It is a complete understanding of the universe, why it is as and why it exists at all.

845. People who boast about their IQ are losers.

846. I'm not afraid of death, but I'm in no hurry to die.

847. Exploration by real people inspire us.

848. Quite people have the loudest minds.

849. We are just an advanced breed of monkeys on a minor planet of a very average star. But we can understand the Universe. That makes us something very special.

850. My expectations were reduced to zero when I was 21 after I was diagnosed with motor-neurons disease. Everything since then has been a bonus.

86
Steve Jobs

851. Innovation distinguishes between a leader and a follower.

852. Everyone here has the sense that right now is one of those moments when we are influencing the future.

853. My favorite things in life don't cost any money.

854. Some people aren't used to an environment where excellence is expected.

855. Sometimes when you innovate, you make mistakes. It is best to admit them quickly, and get on with improving your other innovations.

856. Things don't have to change the world to be important.

857. I want to be the best, not the biggest.

858. Older people ask, "What is it?" but the children ask, "What can I do with it?"

859. It's not a faith in technology. It's faith in people.

860. I tried to intersect technology and art.

87
Sun Tzu

861. If you know the enemy and know yourself, you need not fear a hundred battles.

862. Regard your soldiers as your children, and they will follow you into the deepest valleys; look on them as your own beloved sons, and they will stand by you even unto death.

863. The opportunity to secure ourselves against defeat lies in our own hands, but the opportunity of defeating the enemy is provided by the enemy himself.

864. He who knows when he can fight and when he cannot, will be victorious.

865. The quality of decision is like the well-timed swoop of a falcon which enables it to strike and destroy its victim.

866. Pretend inferiority and encourage his arrogance.

867. Be extremely subtle, even to the point of formlessness. Be extremely mysterious, even to the point of soundlessness. Thereby you can be the director of the opponent's fate.

868. Do not attack the enemy, attack the enemy's strategy.

869. He who is prudent and lies in wait for an enemy who is not will win.

870. There is no instance of a nation benefitting from a prolonged warfare.

88
Sylvia Plath

871. If you expect nothing from anybody, you're never disappointed.

872. The worst enemy to creativity is self-doubt.

873. I shut my eyes and all the world drops dead; I lift my eyes and all is born again.

874. If neurotic is wanting two mutually exclusive things at one and the same time, then I'm neurotic as hell. I'll be flying back and forth between one mutually exclusive thing and another for the rest of my days.

875. If I have not the power to out myself in the place of other people, but must be continually burrowing inward, I shall never be the magnanimous creative person I wish to be. Yet I am hypnotized by the workings of the individual alone, and am continually using myself as a specimen

876. Perhaps when we fin ourselves wanting everything, it is because we are dangerously close to wanting nothing.

877. Wear your heart on your skin in this life.

878. What I want back is what I was.

879. What a man is is an arrow into the future, and what a woman is is the place the arrow shoots off from.

880. Is there no way out of the mind?

89
Tennessee Williams

881. For time is the longest distance between two places.

882. We have to distrust each other. It is our only defense against betrayal.

883. There is a time for departure even when there's no certain place to go.

884. Luck is believing you're lucky.

885. Life is an unanswered question, but let's sill believe in the importance of that question.

886. We are all sentenced to solitary confinement inside our own skins, for life.

887. Success is blocked by concentrating on it.

888. Success is shy – it wont come out while you're watching.

889. We all live in a house on fire, no fire department to call; no way out, just the

upstairs window to look out of while the fire burns the house with us trapped, locked in it.

890. I have always depended on the kindness of strangers.

90
Thomas Acquinas

891. The things that we love tell us what we are.

892. To one who has faith, no explanation is necessary. To one without faith, no explanation is possible.

893. Men cannot live without joy, therefore when he is deprived of joys, it is necessary that he become addicted to carnal pleasures.

894. If the highest aim of a captain were to preserve his ship, he would keep it in port forever.

895. Without friends, even the most agreeable pursuits become tedious.

896. Man should not consider his material possession his own, but as common to all, so as to share them without hesitation when others are in need.

897. Good can exist without evil but evil cannot exist without good.

898. Not everything that is more difficult is more meritorious.

899. We can't have full knowledge all at once.

900. Love takes up where knowledge leaves off.

91
Thomas Edison

901. The most certain way to succeed is always to try just one more time.

902. Opportunity is missed by most people because it is dressed in overalls and looks like work.

903. There's a better way to do it, find it.

904. To invent, you need a good imagination and a pile of junk.

905. I have friends in overalls whose friendship I would not swap for the favor of the kings of the world.

906. I never did a day's work in my life. It was all fun.

907. I never did anything by accident, they came by work.

908. The value of an idea lies in the using of it.

909. To have a great idea, have a lot of them.

910. The chief function of the body is to carry the brain around.

92
Thomas Jefferson

911. Nothing can stop the hero, nothing can help the fool.

912. In matters of style, swim with the current; in matters of principle, stand like a rock.

913. I like the dreams of the future better than the history of the past.

914. Banks are more dangerous than armies.

915. Do not bite at the bait of pleasure, till you know there is no hook beneath it.

916. Better to have no ideas that false ones.

917. It does me no injury for my neighbor to say there are twenty god or no God.

918. One travels more useful when alone, because he reflects more.

919. One loves to possess arms, though they hope never to have occasion for them.

920. Whenever you do a thing, act as if all the world were watching.

93
T.S. Eliot

921. We shall not cease from exploration, and the end of all our exploring will be to arrive where we started and know the place for the first time.

922. Only those who will risk going too far can possibly find out how far one can go.

923. If you aren't in over your head, how do you know how tall you are?

924. Poetry is not a turning loose of emotion, but an escape from emotion.

925. Only those who have personality and emotions know what it means to want to escape from these things.

926. Where is the knowledge we have lost in information?

927. This is the way the world ends, not with a bang, but a whimper.

928. Half of the harm that is doesn't in this world is due to people who want to feel

important. They don't mean to do harm. But the harm does not interest them.

929. Deliver me from the man of excellent intention and impure heart: for the heart is deceitful above all things, and desperately wicked.

930. Anxiety is the hand maiden of creativity.

94
Vincent Van Gogh

931. Great things are done by a series of small things brought together.

932. You can't get up until you fall.

933. I dream of painting and then I paint my dream.

934. What would life be if we had no courage to attempt anything.

935. Poetry surrounds us everywhere, but putting it on paper is not so easy as looking at it.

936. Conscience is a man's compass.

937. There may be a great fire in our hearts, yet no one ever comes to warm himself at it, and the passerby's see only a wisp of smoke.

938. I wish they would only take me as I am.

939. I see drawings and pictures in the poorest of huts and the dirtiest of corners.

940. A good picture is equivalent to a good deed.

95
Virgil

941. It never troubles the wolf how many the sheep may be.

942. They succeed because they think they can.

943. The sweetest hours fly fastest.

944. I fear those who bring gifts.

945. Endure the present and watch for better things.

946. It is easy to go down into Hell: but to climb back again, to retrace one's steps to the upper air – there's the rub.

947. Trust not too much to appearances.

948. Each of us bears his own Hell.

949. The world cares very little what you know but you are able to do counts.

950. Rage supplies enemies with weapons.

96
Voltaire

951. It is difficult to free fools from the chains they revere.

952. The progress of rivers to the ocean is not so rapid as that of man to error.

953. Judge a man by his questions rather than his answers.

954. Is there anyone so wise as to learn by the experience of others?

955. What is tolerance? It is the consequence of humanity. We are all formed of frailty, let us pardon reciprocally each other's folly – that is the first law of nature.

956. Every man is guilty of all the good he did not do.

957. To succeed in the world it is not enough to be stupid, you must also be well-mannered.

958. Love is a canvas furnished by nature and embroidered by imagination.

959. It is vain for the coward to flee; death follows close behind; it is only by defying it that the brave escape.

960. A witty saying proves nothing.

97
Walt Disney

961. It's fun to do the impossible.

962. Quit talking and begin doing.

963. A kick in the teeth may be the best thing in the world. All the adversity I've had in my life, all my troubles and obstacles, have strengthened me.

964. I only hope that we don't lose sight of one thing – that it was all started by a mouse.

965. Of all of our inventions for mass communication, pictures still speak the most universally understood language.

966. Time and conditions change so rapidly that we must keep our aim constantly focused on the future.

967. Mickey Mouse popped out of my mind onto a drawing pad 20 years ago on a train ride from Manhattan to Hollywood at a time when business fortunes of my brother Roy

and myself were at lowest ebb and disaster seemed right around the corner.

968. When you believe in a thing, believe in it unquestionably.

969. Never neglect your family for business.

970. There is more treasure in books than in all the pirate's loot on Treasure Island.

98
William S. Burroughs

971. In deep sadness, there is no place for sentimentality.

972. Your mind will answer most questions if you learn to relax and wait for the answer.

973. Sometimes paranoia's just having all the facts.

974. After one look at this planet, any visitor from space would say, "I want to see the manager."

975. The face of evil is always the face of total need.

976. Nothing is true, everything is permitted.

977. The aim of education is the knowledge, not of facts, but of values.

978. You must learn to exist with no religion, no country, no allies.

979. Desperation is the raw material of drastic change. Only those who can leave

behind everything they have ever believed in can hope to escape.

980. Artists to my mind are the real architects of change, and not the political legislators who implement change after the fact.

99
William Shakespeare

981. We know what we are, but know not what we may be.

982. Love all, trust a few, do wrong to none.

983. Better three hours too soon than a minute too late.

984. The course of true love never did run smooth.

985. God gave you one face, and you make yourself another.

986. A fool thinks himself to be wise, but a wise man knows himself to be a fool.

987. Suspicion always haunts the guilty mind.

988. The empty vessel makes the loudest sound.

989. Listen to many, speak to a few.

990. What is past is prologue.

100
Winston Churchill

991. Success consists of going from failure to failure without loss of enthusiasm.

992. Courage is what it takes to stand up and speak; courage is also what it takes to sit down and listen.

993. We make a living by what we get, but we make a life by what we give.

994. The truth is incontrovertible. Malice may attack it, ignorance may deride it, but in the end, there it is.

995. To improve is to change, to be perfect is to change often.

996. However beautiful the strategy, you should occasionally look at the results.

997. History will be kind to me for I intend to write it.

998. Now this is not the end. It is not even the beginning of the end. But it is, perhaps, the end of the beginning.

999. Truth is so precious that she should always be attended by a bodyguard of lies.

1000. It is always wise to look ahead, but difficult to look further than you can see.